BOW WOW BONES

BOW WOW BONES
HOW I GOT MY DOGS

Luke Monin & Family

TATE PUBLISHING
AND ENTERPRISES, LLC

Published by Tate Publishing & Enterprises, LLC
127 E. Trade Center Terrace | Mustang, Oklahoma 73064 USA
1.888.361.9473 | www.tatepublishing.com

Tate Publishing is committed to excellence in the publishing industry. The company reflects the philosophy established by the founders, based on Psalm 68:11,
"The Lord gave the word and great was the company of those who published it."

Book design copyright © 2013 by Tate Publishing, LLC. All rights reserved.
Cover design by Joseph Emnace
Interior design by Gram Telen

Published in the United States of America

ISBN: 978-1-62902-854-5
1. Family & Relationships / General
2. Pets / Dogs / General
13.10.31

DEDICATION

Our family would like to dedicate this book to the Faulkner County Humane Society. Their mission is to place homeless pets into their forever homes. Also, to all of those lost hound dogs or pets out there looking for a loving forever home. May you be a blessing to them.

TABLE OF CONTENTS

INTRODUCTION

....

This story begins with a family that had no hope of *ever* having a pet, let alone two dogs and a fish. But more about that later.

I am the mother of two beautiful boys, Luke, age ten, and Ethan, age five. I'm also the mother of Rocky, our eleven-year-old Australian shepherd, or at least partly, a three-year-old Jack Russell terrier named Lucky, and a Beta fish named Nomad.

Did I mention to you that I am their mommy? They all look to me to be their main caregiver—mainly for food, a hug, or a good belly rub.

My husband is the one that told me that under no uncertain terms that dogs are dirty and that we would *never* have one! He, unfortunately, waited until after we were married to share this. I was devastated because I grew up with my dog Killer for sixteen years. She was a golden retriever-German shepherd mix, all golden yellow with blue eyes and a bright-blue collar.

Killer was an inside dog that I could share all of my troubles with, have fun with, and she was my best friend. Once I had the flu for a week and I couldn't get off the couch, and she stayed right there with me until I was better.

One day my brother, sister, and I taught Killer how to climb a ladder, which came back to bite us later. Our parents had given us the task of washing all of the windows on the first floor of our house. We were good workers and had grown to make games out of our many jobs.

My dad had a motorcycle shed attached to the back of the house. It was much easier to climb a short ladder to get up there to do the back of the house windows. Killer kept us company, and one of us had the brilliant idea that Killer could join us up there on top of that shed.

So we carefully took each paw and put them on each rung of the ladder and taught her how to climb. Killer was a very smart dog, so she caught on very quickly.

So our game began. We would call her to come up the ladder, she would smile, and up she would come. We would let her in the window and back out the side door. Oh, we laughed, and Killer seemed to enjoy it too. The day went by quickly, and before we knew it, all of the windows were sparkling clean.

Unfortunately, my parents had a new roof put on shortly after that, and Killer climbed up and started barking like crazy at the workers. My dad had to climb up on top of a three-story double house to carry her back down to the ground.

Needless to say my dad was not pleased. We learned two important lessons that day: one, dogs should not learn how to climb ladders; and two, you should not wash triple-track windows with a hose. Oops!

Killer was like most dogs when it came to the mailman. She absolutely hated the mailman, even though we tried to make friends. The mailman would have to come into our entryway each day to put our mail into our box, and poor Killer would be home all by herself. She would start leaping and jumping to bark at him. One time she shredded Mom's curtains to bits, and she ended up in the doghouse.

Another time she even ran halfway up a tree chasing a cat before she realized that dogs can't climb trees.

So you can see why I was so devastated when my husband said, "No pets!"

We eventually inherited Rocky, our Australian shepherd, from my brother-in-law, Mark. He was moving from Arkansas to Arizona, and he knew that Rocky was an outside dog and that he would not do well traveling in a car for 1,300 miles.

Let me tell you something about Rocky. He will *not* come into the house, no matter what the circumstance. Once Mark tried to carry him into the house during an ice storm, and he fought him with all of his might. And he still would not come in.

My husband, Matt, had to say yes to his best friend and brother when he was asked to give Rocky a home.

Matt would complain, "I have to go outside in the cold and feed the dog."

Then I would say, affectionately, "His name is Rocky." Eventually, I could hear him talking to Rocky and see him rubbing his belly with his foot. I think Matt was okay with Rocky because he was an outside dog.

Lucky, on the other hand, is our very active Jack Russell terrier that found us in January of 2007. It was a cold winter day, and he was just a tiny pup. He stopped by to play with the kids in the driveway. Somehow he ended up in our house, but I will let Luke share his story later.

I do want to add one important fact about Lucky. He is the only dog that could have ever survived in the Monin home. He is a smart hound dog, and he knows how to work the system to get what he wants, which is food and a warm place to sleep—and believe me, he likes both of those. The most important, however, is love. We feel like he was sent to us as a gift from God.

So here begins Luke's story *Bow Wow Bones: How I Got My Dogs*. I hope you truly love it!

HOW ROCKY WAS FOUND

Hello. My name is Luke Monin, and I am ten years old, and I wanted to share with you how I got my dogs.

My brother Ethan and I hoped and prayed for a pet of our very own, one that we could love, play with, and grow up with, but Dad said, "No pets!"

Rocky was our very first pet that was our very own. He is our best friend and hound dog that we can play with every day. So let's begin our story with how Rocky was found.

One day in 1997, my uncle Mark's friend, Jeff, was on Black Snake Mountain in Hot Springs, Arkansas, when he saw two pups in a ditch by the side of the road. He gave one to his best friend and my uncle, Mark, who named his puppy Rocky, after Rocky Road ice cream. Jeff took the other one home and named it Cocoa.

Rocky was fast for such a little pup and refused to be caught. Jeff had to chase Rocky through the woods to finally catch him. I guess you could say that he was a little stubborn.

LUKE MONIN & FAMILY

Mark thinks that Rocky may have been abused, and that is why he was afraid to get caught and also why he refuses to come into the house. We may never know what happened to Rocky before he came to our family, but we are just happy that Rocky is here with us now.

After the puppies were found, they took the dogs to their new homes. Both Mark and Jeff had a fenced yard, so they each had room for a dog.

At that time, Mark was a bachelor and lived in Arkansas until he married and moved with his beautiful bride to Arizona. But that is another story for another day.

Cocoa didn't last long because he became mean, and they had to put him to sleep, but Rocky still lives on and on.

Rocky is an Australian shepherd mix that's mostly white and black, and he has brown spots on his paws.

THE BIG MOVE: PART 1

It was a cool, crisp winter day that New Year's Eve in 2002. To Rocky, it was just another day at the homestead. He was happy to lie in the warmth of the sunshine and just enjoy the morning air. Rocky didn't know it yet, but today would be moving day for Mark, his bride, and for him. He woke up and barked at a few people that passed by, but for the most part he seemed content.

Meanwhile, my uncle Mark and his bride were hustling and bustling in the house, running in and out carrying box after box out to their cars. The phone kept ringing, and everyone that stopped by seemed like they were in a really big hurry too. Cars kept pulling in and out of each driveway, and some people parked in the street or in front of Mark's house.

One thing I always found interesting about Mark's house was that it had two driveways. I always thought that was really neat. I guess you could say it was a "his" and "her" driveway, one for Mark and one for his bride. Or it could be two cars in one driveway and the Old Boy in the other.

The Old Boy was a 1969 Black Ford truck that was in rough shape, but it was in Mark's price range, which was a very small range at that time.

Many people laughed at him or just thought he was just plain crazy to buy such an old truck to fix up, let alone to drive. It had three on the tree, which meant it only had three speeds and you had to shift it on the column. I know my dad has a Nissan truck that he loves, and he certainly does not shift it from the steering wheel; he shifts it like anyone that drives a standard.

So the Old Boy was special. He had spirit and had even been known to drive across the country from as far as New York to Arkansas or anywhere in between. At least that is what I have learned from listening to my dad and Mark tell stories.

My dad is a great storyteller. He likes to share stories about crazy things that family members have done, and he has the heartiest laugh you have ever heard. Anyone that hears my dad laugh feels compelled to laugh even if they don't think it's funny.

Ah yes, my dad is a great storyteller. My brother Ethan and I can't get enough of his stories, and we often have him tell them over and over again. I have to believe they are all true, and my dad says one day he will tell me the unedited version when I'm eighteen. I am not sure what that means exactly, but I am looking forward to turning eighteen in about eight years.

THE BIG MOVE: PART 2

Moving day was a very exciting day for Mark. He would be starting a new chapter in his life—moving to a new state, starting a new and exciting job, one that paid more money and offered more opportunity—but it was also a very sad day.

He knew today would be the day that he and his friend Rocky would have to say good-bye. Mark knew that he would see Rocky every time he visited, but he knew life together would never be the same.

So with a heavy heart, he gave Rocky one last belly rub, scratched him behind the ears, and talked to him only the way a master could talk to his beloved friend and dog.

I was not there that day. I was at home waiting for our family to finally have a dog of our very own. I knew it would be an exciting day for our family. I guess I didn't think about Mark being sad. In my mind, he always looked so happy; maybe he was just always glad to see me and play with me and my brother.

I like to think Mark's talk with Rocky went something like this:

"Rocky, today you are going to live with my brother Matt and his family. It will be your new home. Don't think that I don't love you. This will be for your own good. I wish I could take you with me, but I know this will be better for you."

So after the good-byes were all said and done, the fun part began: catching Rocky and putting him into his dog porter. A dog porter is basically a plastic box with a metal rack for a front door. This particular porter was just a hair too small for Rocky.

Rocky was no small fellow, not sure if you remember this or not, but Rocky does *not* like to go inside anywhere, let alone a house, a car, a shed, and definitely not a porter!

So how was Mark going to get Rocky to go inside of the porter, get him into the car, and then drive him for an hour and a half to his new home?

Mark had a plan. It seemed like a good plan until he tried to put it into action. Rocky had this gift—or should I call it a sixth sense; it was almost like he had a built in rearview mirror. He knew that Mark was trying to catch him and would probably kill him if he did.

So Rocky, ever so swift and talented, just kept a step or two ahead of Mark. Mark would get closer, and Rocky would still be just a little bit ahead of him. Enough where he could almost touch him but far enough away where he would never be caught.

So the chase began. Mark would speed up, and then Rocky would speed up. Mark would slow down a bit, and Rocky would slow down a bit until they made it all the way around the perimeter of the yard. Mark realized this was not working, so he had his bride close in from the opposite direction.

You would have thought that Rocky was a greased pig; he slipped through their grasps many times before he was finally cornered. Mark made the grab, and oh, Rocky squirmed and jerked and tried with all of his might to break Mark's tight hold, but Mark was strong and had a good, tight squeeze on him.

Somehow he managed to carry him to the porter, but the porter was lying flat, and Mark knew he couldn't hold Rocky much longer. Rocky was a fighter; fear took hold of him, and he wouldn't and just couldn't go into that mean old porter. He didn't want to hurt his master, but he certainly didn't like being caught.

Mark yelled to his bride, "Flip the porter up so I can put Rocky in from the top instead of the side!" So she did, and Mark dropped Rocky into the porter before he could get away.

Rocky was trapped; he had been caught. He complained and tried scratching at the door, but it was no use. His heartbeat was racing a mile a minute, and all was lost. The terrible sounds of Rocky trying to get out broke Mark's heart, but he knew it had to be done.

All was packed, and the porter with his trusted friend inside had to be lifted together by both Mark and his bride to get his porter into the back seat of Mark's classic 1986 red Mustang.

So Rocky was jostled a bit back and forth until his porter settled into its resting-place. It was a very scary moment for Rocky; he thought for sure that was it, that he would certainly be killed or something terrible would happen to him.

The drive took an hour and a half.

Rocky was still trying to move in his porter that was just a hair too small for him. Finally, he settled down and panted. Moisture dripped from his tongue, his heart still beating fast, but perhaps a little bit slower since he had to accept the fact that he had been caught.

By the time Mark pulled into our driveway, we had been waiting for what seemed like hours for him to get there. We looked window to window, ran outside several times thinking he was here with our first ever dog that was going to be our very own, but it was always a false alarm.

Finally, Mark pulled into the driveway, and we came running out to greet him and to especially say hello to Rocky. Rocky was chomping at the bit to get out of his mean old porter. So Mark parked the car closer to the fence, and Daddy and Mark hoisted Rocky's porter out of the mustang.

They carried Rocky's porter with Rocky trembling inside carefully until he was safely nestled into his new home, our backyard. We made sure the fence was closed before we opened the door of Rocky's porter.

He came out like a shot! He immediately started sniffing and inspecting the yard. We tried to pet him, but he was not ready for that level of affection yet.

Plus, I think Rocky was mad at Mark because at first he would not even look at him. We were all worried that Rocky would not like his new home even though it was much bigger than Mark's old yard.

The only home Rocky ever knew before this was Mark's yard. He rarely if ever left the yard, so Mark's yard and his master were mostly what Rocky knew before he ended up here at our house. Don't get me wrong. Rocky was happy at Mark's house, and he would give us that sweet smile when we would come to visit him, so we knew he was a happy dog.

Now Rocky's life had been turned upside down; he would have children chasing him wanting to play with him and keeping him busy. No more of those lazy days with little human contact. So we all prayed and hoped that Rocky would be happy in his new home.

WHAT I THINK HAPPENED TO ROCKY

Hello. My name is Ethan. I'm Luke's five-year-old brother, and this is what I think happened to Rocky. If you don't listen to this one, you will be sad. You will want to hear what I think happened to Rocky.

I think Rocky had owners who were nice, and his mom was keeping up with him, but he was always going to explore somewhere.

He couldn't believe his eyes when he saw lots of stuff like swing sets and kids—and he loved the kids. He didn't know what they were, but they all looked fun. So every day he and his brother, the other pup, would play together on the stuff.

Once, he was swinging and didn't know what was happening, and he jumped off the swing, landed on a trampoline, and bounced up so high that he landed in a tree. One of the kids caught him, and he was happy for that kid to hold him because he loved that kid and he always fed him a nice plate of milk. Remember, Rocky was just a pup, and babies do like milk.

Rocky and his brother were the two pups that weren't bought. One day the owners had to put him and his brother on the side of the road because they couldn't afford to keep them all. Rocky's Mom was sad and was sold to someone else.

Rocky always had his brother with him until one day someone caught him, and he wasn't ready to be caught. Then they put him in a car, and the car the car had spots on it. Rocky looked at the car, and it looked beautiful, but he didn't want to be caught or certainly to go inside of that car or anywhere.

Bye, this is Ethan all you friends I'm glad that you listened to me. I hope you enjoyed my story. I'm glad you listened to me or you would have missed it and been sad and I am going, bye now…Have a nice day!

KIDS VERSUS DOGS

Hello, this is Luke's mom again! Luke asked me to write this chapter called "Kids versus Dogs," so here it goes.

I am continuously surprised by the similarities between our dogs and our children. Our family has one big old dog, Rocky, and one small active dog, Lucky. We have two children, Luke, who is our almost eleven-year-old and is about four foot six, and his brother Ethan, who is our five-year-old and about three foot six. My husband says we have a monkey and a gorilla because one is so much bigger than the other.

Luke has a great sense of humor and gets all of his Mamaw's jokes, but he does have a serious manner about him. I believe he is a very deep thinker. He loves to read books and has opened a library in his room.

Rocky, our older dog, will come up to you, smile, get a good scratching behind the ears, and then he is done and ready to move on. He moves kind of slow, but he can still catch birds when he wants to. You can always count on Rocky for a smile.

Ethan is a very active five-year-old. When he was younger, he would try to get Luke to play with him by jumping on his head, but Luke had no interest; he just wanted to read his books. Ethan is the type of guy who loves to dance, sing, and hunt for bad guys around the house. He hasn't learned how to read yet, so he is all about action and having fun!

Lucky is our very excitable Jack Russell terrier. He likes to run around the yard at top speed, loves to chase a ball, and loves to play.

Lucky would leap and jump at Rocky's snout and would want to play with him, but all he really wanted was to just be left alone. Rocky would just put his paw on Lucky to hold him down, until he would eventually give up.

In closing, Luke and Rocky are like our "old men" in the family. Luke once played a wise old owl in a play at church. Needless to say, the part was made for him.

Luke and Rocky are the wise old men in our family—adorable but a little serious, and deep thinkers. Ethan and Lucky love to play and wish the two old dogs would play with them.

All are special in their own ways, and all bring their gifts to our family.

HOW LUCKY CAME TO US

....

Hi, this is Luke again, and I wanted to share Lucky's tale as I remember it.

One day, on January 16th to be exact, my friends and I were playing in the front yard when out of nowhere on the street was this little puppy. He saw us and came up our driveway. We played with him until my mom called us in for snack.

On the way inside the door, the puppy ran into the house and into my parents' bedroom before we could stop him. He even peed on the rug. Mom didn't like that part very much and really didn't want him to think this was his home. We picked him up and put him outside of the front door. He ran off, and we thought we would never see him again.

That night, my mom had gone to a party and stopped by the grocery store on the way home. When she returned, she saw him, and he was freezing cold.

Mom had backed up her car to the front door to unload the groceries from her trunk and had called Daddy outside to help her. Meanwhile, the little puppy that was no bigger than a beanbag came joyfully running up to her. He was shaking because he was freezing cold.

The average temperature in January where we live is about twenty-four degrees.

My mom said to my dad, "I think this is the little puppy from earlier today. We can't just leave him out here to freeze."

So my dad said, "Okay, just for tonight we will put him in the backyard with Rocky, but in the morning, we will have to look for his owner. Remember, he is *not* our dog."

So they put him in the backyard with a box to sleep in and worried that Rocky might not like the idea of having an uninvited guest staying in the backyard with him, so they kept their ears open and checked on them both several times before going to bed.

The next day, we put up flyers around town that said "Found: Jack Russell terrier Puppy." A week went by, and nothing happened. We went to the Greenbrier Super Center, but our posters had been taken down. So after that our dad said we could keep him.

We didn't know when we woke up that cold sixteenth day of January that it would truly be our family's "Lucky" day. And that is how Lucky got his name.

Daddy didn't want us to name him Lucky because Rocky and Lucky sounded too similar, and he thought the dogs wouldn't know whom we were calling. But the name stuck, and Lucky became his name.

WHEN LUCKY MET HIS MATCH

....

This is Luke again, and I am chomping at the bit to share the story of how Lucky met his match.

In the spring of 2007, there was an especially odd day, not just because of the weather. It was early April and was almost 80 degrees, which is unusual even for Arkansas. It was also a special day because it was the day Lucky met his match.

It started off as any ordinary day. We went to school as usual. Then, when we returned home, we started playing with the hounds. Then this strange puppy that looked just like Lucky appeared out of nowhere. He looked just like Lucky except he had a stump tail, so we knew he was either a Jack Russell terrier or a rat terrier.

He was so cute, and we named him Peanut because he was as small as a peanut. It was almost like we had twins from the same litter. Lucky and Peanut ran and chased each other, tumbled in the grass, and played and played. Oh, what fun it was for all of us.

We couldn't believe our luck that we were being blessed with yet another dog that found us!

So we called Mommy out to come see, and she had to rub her eyes and do a double take. The first thing she said was, "Don't fall in love with him. We already have two dogs. Daddy will never go for this!"

So we watched them play and had so much fun with the two puppies. We even have a picture for our memory book so we will never forget Peanut.

Mom grabbed the baby stroller from the garage and put Peanut in the baby seat. She didn't put the seat belt on him because she didn't want to hurt him.

So we walked up and down our street asking everyone if Peanut was their puppy. She knew under no uncertain terms that Daddy would *not* go for being the owners of three dogs. We were already pushing our luck with two.

Finally, we turned on to Pinto Trail and ran into two beautiful twin girls who went to our school, and they came running up to us, saying, "You found him!" They said his name was Harvey.

We were happy to give them the puppy but a bit sad. It would have been fun to watch Lucky and Peanut—I mean Harvey—play every day in our yard. We told them to bring him by to play, but they never did.

DADDY'S THOUGHTS

....

This is Daddy, and when Luke asked me to write this chapter, I must confess that I struggled with what to say about our pets good and bad.

I must preface all of my thoughts by reiterating what has been frequently stated about me throughout this story. I am not a dog person. I still am not a dog person. More specifically, I am simply not an animal person.

I don't wish animals in general any harm, and I strongly want to see any animal live its life in the way it chooses—just not around me. If some see this as a character flaw, so be it, but I make no excuses for who I am.

That said, I do truly like our dogs, but I also don't like them as though they were people. They are not people, but they are a responsibility that one accepts when choosing to have a pet in his or her life.

Pets are not capable of caring or providing for themselves, and I detest people who knowingly treat an animal poorly or, even worse, cruelly. If you can't treat them well, don't choose to have a pet in your life. That is a choice, pure and simple.

Our dogs came to us by very different routes, as has been explained. I was happy to have Rocky come to us and have also enjoyed the ancillary benefit of having our backyard fenced in as part of taking him in.

It does pain me to realize that Rocky is getting quite old and that he is moving very slowly these days. He does remain protective of us as much as he can, but he doesn't move around much anymore, and he spends most of his time lying in the shade.

He doesn't seem to be in any pain but realizes that he just doesn't have the energy to get up and go anymore. He's still a good old dog, and it breaks my heart to know the reality that he's in the twilight of his days.

Lucky, on the other hand, still has plenty of energy but uses it sparingly. He too likes to lay in the shade and sleep, sometimes sleeping outside during the day, and then all night long in his porter in our family room.

He is always very good while in the house and doesn't get into things he doesn't belong in. He does sometimes nose around the garbage can by my chair, so I have to be careful not to leave food garbage in there.

There are limits to self-control in a dog that is always hungry for people food. I understand that and don't hold it against him. He's a nice dog, but he has to know his limits. It seems like he forgets those limits and begins to think that he is one of the kids. Sometimes I have to remind him that he is not. I am firm with him but not mean, and he gets my point quickly.

There are other times though when he is good to have around, such as when storms are in the area. We can always tell just how bad it's going to get based on Lucky's reaction. He's more effective than a weather radio because he senses when it's getting bad in Greenbrier, not just in the county in general.

They are both good dogs and have become part of the family whether I initially liked it or not. They make Tracy [Mommy] and the boys happy, and it is comforting to have them around since homes with dogs are less likely to be burgled. Overall, they do the job of rounding out our household nicely, and I am happy to have them around, though I am still not a dog person.

This is Luke's mom again. I truly believe that something has changed in Daddy since our pets have come to us.

When Rocky first came to live with us, Daddy tolerated him because he knew that we all were so excited to have Rocky here with us and to finally have a pet of our very own. Also, he knew Rocky needed a good home and that it would help his best friend and brother to move on to the next chapter in his life knowing that Rocky was taken care of.

But has something really changed in Daddy? I say, "Thou doth protest too much." That means that Daddy does like also being the daddy of two boys and two dogs. It gives him the security to know that we are taken care of even when he has to work out of town.

I do want to back up my story with something that actually happened just a few weeks ago.

Daddy and I were driving down an old country road when we drove past a turtle. Daddy exclaimed, "Was that turtle upside down?"

I was just looking at the rolling hills and the beautiful countryside, so I did not notice. I told Daddy to turn around and head back to check on that turtle. So we made a three-point turn and headed back.

In Arkansas every spring, I affectionately call it "turtle season"; that is when all of the turtles try to cross the road to mate. Many of them do not make it, but the ones that do, we cheer for as we drive by and say, "He made it!"

So we headed back to that poor turtle stuck on its back, and Daddy was all set to flip him back over, and that is when we noticed that turtle did not make it.

We both hung our heads down low and agreed that at least we tried, but Daddy was willing to make a difference in that turtle's life.

So has something changed? I will let you decide for yourself.

CONCLUSION

So ends our story of *Bow Wow Bones: How I Got My Dogs*. You can see how a family that had no hope of *ever* having a dog now lives in harmony with two dogs.

We hope this story gives hope to all of those children out there that wished, hoped, and prayed that one day they would have a dog of their very own too.

This is Luke's mom again, and yes, I say only two dogs because while this story was being written, our beta fish, Nomad, didn't make it to the end. He was red, white, and yellow all over with a little bit of black on his tail fin.

Luke had dreamed of having a fish of his very own, just like he had dreamed of having a dog of his very own.

So he saved his allowance and convinced us, which was no easy task considering how his dad had strong feelings against having animals in the house. But Dad finally said that he would at least think about letting him have a fish. So in Luke's language that meant a yes, or at least a strong maybe.

Dad asked questioningly, "Who is going feed the fish?" Luke proclaimed that he would feed the fish every day.

I asked, "Who would take care of the fish when we go on vacation?"

Luke had an answer for everything. He said that his friend and neighbor Gracie would be happy to take care of our fish anytime we needed her to. Luke also said that we could simply take his bowl to her house for a week and that her parents wouldn't mind.

So Luke saved his allowance and drove us crazy until we finally said he could go and at least look at the fish. Luke looked for a yellow fish because yellow was his favorite color.

I didn't think any of the fish looked particularly healthy and wondered how you knew if it was a boy or a girl fish. I secretly hoped he would pick a girl fish because I am outnumbered with all boys in the family.

All of the fish were in individual containers so you could easily look at each one. Luke zeroed in on a yellow Beta fish in a cup labeled "Male Beta Fish."

I tried to talk him out of it. I even said, "How about this one right here, this purple Beta Fish?" I had my heart set on it and highly encouraged Luke to pick that one, but I knew that in the end he would want to pick a yellow fish because ever since he was a little boy he would always choose yellow in everything.

When Luke was learning how to talk, he would say "yelldow." We all thought it was adorable!

So Nomad made his home on our kitchen counter next to the sink. Luke and Ethan fought over who would feed him. Ethan would whine and complain and say, "But Luke did it last time!" and Luke would say, "But he is *my fish*!" So they had to settle on taking turns each day.

Nomad's bowl had to be cleaned once a week to keep it freshened up. Mom first had to catch him, which was like catching Rocky. That fish was so smart that he knew she was trying to catch him and would probably kill him. So he would swim so fast that he would always be on the opposite side of the bowl from Mom.

She would yell out, "Come on! Get into the cup!"

To catch Nomad, Mom would simply take a small coffee cup and dip it into his bowl and try to have the water suck him into the cup to catch him. Nomad was ever so quick and would give her a run for her money.

One time Mom was cleaning Nomad's bowl and, oops, she dropped it into the sink and *smashed* it!

Luckily, Nomad was safely in another bowl at the time, and she ended up putting him in some kind of pedestal bowl that was meant to hold a big candle. Instead of a candle, it became Nomad's second home.

So Nomad had won our family's hearts like Rocky and Lucky did and became part of our family. Watching him swim around his bowl made us all feel so happy.

Mom worried about what would happen if Nomad didn't make it because fish have a very short life span, but she didn't ever mention it to us. She wanted us to be able to enjoy Nomad for however long he was with us.

So you can see that even though some families have no hope of *ever* having a dog, life happens. Mark didn't think he would ever live in Arkansas or Arizona when he was growing up. All he knew was that he liked the way those southern girls talked and that one day he would marry one. I think one of the reasons Mark fell in love with his bride was because of the way she said "dawg" instead of dog.

So ends our story of Rocky, Lucky, Nomad, Mark, and his beautiful bride.

Mark now has a new dog, and her name is Greta. She is a really big German Shepard that his kids can probably ride on if they wanted too. She is gentle and a great watchdog but can never take the place of Rocky in his heart.

For when you have a best friend and beloved pet, he stays in your heart forever. Things will happen in your life where you will remember fondly the memories that you have made together.

So hope is out there for all you who would love to have a dog or a pet of your very own. So pray, keep your room clean, and keep your eyes open, for one day will truly be your "Lucky" day, too!